Thi book
7 DAY
BOO!

FOR
REFERENCE ONLY

KT-432-608

PLAY IN EARLY CHILDHOOD

Play and development are key topics for all who work with young children. Based on the pioneering work of Mary D. Sheridan, *Play in Early Childhood: From Birth to Six Years* is an introductory text which explains how children's play develops and how they develop as they play.

Play in Early Childhood features

- over eighty illustrations
- descriptions of play at each stage of development, from birth to six years
- outlines of different play sequences
- children with special needs
- the adult's role in providing for play

This second edition has been thoroughly revised and updated to meet the needs of early years workers and students on courses leading to awards in children's care and education.

Mary D. Sheridan was a researcher in child development for over forty years, and is the author of the best-selling book *From Birth to Five Years*, also published by Routledge.

Jackie Harding is a primary school head teacher and author, and **Liz Meldon-Smith** is an early years consultant and author.

GC 072672   GRIMSBY COLLEGE

PLAY IN EARLY CHILDHOOD
From birth to six years

Mary D. Sheridan

Revised and updated by

Jackie Harding and **Liz Meldon-Smith**

LIBRARY

London and New York

First published 1977 by the NFER Publishing Company
Reprinted 1985, 1987, 1988, 1989, 1990, 1991

Reprinted 1993, 1996, and second edition first published 1999
by Routledge
11 New Fetter Lane, London EC4P 4EE

Reprinted 2002

Routledge is an imprint of the Taylor & Francis Group

© 1977, 1999 the estate of Mary D. Sheridan

Typeset in Sabon, Frutiger 45 and Sassoon Primary by Routledge
Printed and bound in Great Britain by TJ International Ltd, Padstow,
Cornwall

All rights reserved. No part of this book may be reprinted or reproduced
or utilized in any form or by any electronic, mechanical, or other means,
now known or hereafter invented, including photocopying and
recording, or in any information storage or retrieval system, without
permission in writing from the publishers.

British Library Cataloguing in Publication Data
A catalogue record for this book is available from the British Library

ISBN 0–415–18693–5

Contents

Acknowledgements

The photographs that appear on pp. 5, 8, 9, 45 and 48 were taken by David Robinson with the kind permission of the staff at Heath Clark Nursery, Croydon.

The aims of this section are to:

- explain why the book was originally written
- describe the new edition

THE WORK OF MARY SHERIDAN

The original author of this book is Dr Mary Sheridan, a senior community paediatrician and pioneer in the field of child development. During her lifetime, Mary Sheridan spent many years observing the behaviour of 'real children in real situations'. Her aim was to try to understand how children change as they grow older. Her books, *Spontaneous Play in Early Childhood* and *From Birth to Five Years*, record in words and pictures the results of her observations.

THE NEW EDITION

Since Dr Sheridan wrote *Spontaneous Play in Early Childhood*, a few things have changed, including some of the terminology originally used. While the book was written with psychologists and paediatricians in mind, recently it has been read in increasing numbers by early years workers and others involved in caring for children. As a result the book has been carefully revised and updated to take account of these changes.

THE AIM OF THE BOOK

The aim of the book is to increase readers' knowledge about the nature of play, explain the value of play, and clarify the adult's role in providing for play. It provides a detailed description of children's play from birth to 6 years, including an outline of the elements of spontaneous play in which most children engage during the early years of their lives.

STRUCTURE OF THE BOOK

Much of the original structure of the book has been retained and the text reflects the entitlement of all children to have opportunities to develop through play. A further section has been added, which concerns the role of the adult in providing for play.

The book is arranged as follows:

Section 1:   Definitions relating to play
Section 2:   Ages and stages in the development of play
Section 3:   Outlines of some significant play sequences
Section 4:   Providing for play: The role of adults

A NOTE ABOUT STYLE

For ease of purpose children are referred to as 'she' in the text and as 'he' or 'she' in the illustrations and captions.

Summary

- Mary Sheridan was a pioneer in the study of child development.
- This book gives a detailed description of spontaneous play in the early years.

The aims of this section are to:

- define 'spontaneous play'
- explore the value of play
- explain the role of play in relation to child development
- describe the various functions and types of play
- introduce different theories about play

Definitions

relating to

play

WHAT IS 'SPONTANEOUS PLAY'?

Given the opportunity children play 'spontaneously'. In other words, they provide their own motivation to play and act without prompting or intervention by an adult. The type and duration of the play in which they engage is entirely determined by them and activities can be taken up and stopped at will. To the child, playing is an end in itself and to an observer there may not seem to be any obvious goal or conclusion.

THE VALUE OF PLAY

Just by watching young children it is easy to see that play is often stimulating and rewarding, and that they get a great deal of emotional satisfaction from playing. Although the differences are not always clear-cut or easily understood, it is possible to identify distinct functions that play has for the child. Mary Sheridan termed these functions 'apprenticeship', 'research', 'occupational therapy' and 'recreation'.

Apprenticeship

As they get older, children gradually develop competence in performing everyday tasks, such as dressing and feeding themselves or answering the telephone. Play can provide the means of acquiring and practising such skills.

Research

Children find out about the world around them through a process of observing, exploring, speculating and making discoveries. For example, a child will learn about the properties of water – that some things float and some sink. Playing provides ample opportunity for this kind of informal learning.

Occupational therapy

Play can have a soothing or distracting effect. It can be simply an escape from boredom, a means of diverting attention or coming to terms with things that are physically or emotionally unpleasant, such as pain.

Recreation

This is perhaps the function of play that most readily springs to mind. Children entertain themselves through play. They are simply enjoying themselves and having fun.

PLAY AND DEVELOPMENT

It takes detailed observation over time to see the full value of play. Systematic studies carried out by researchers, including Mary Sheridan, show that the functions that play fulfils for each child from moment-to-moment and day-to-day are part of the wider contribution that play makes to each child's overall development. In other words, playing helps children in their development.

DEVELOPMENT

Development means far more than just growth – it is about gaining and perfecting a whole range of skills and abilities which as adults we take for granted. Children's development comprises a complex mixture of progressive changes which can be broken down and categorised as follows:

- **physical** Children develop increasing control over their movements. This involves *motor skills* (both *gross* and *fine*) and vision. As her vision develops, the child becomes increasingly competent in looking and seeing (far and near). The *fine motor skills* that she develops enable her to manipulate objects, for example tying shoe laces or drawing. *Gross motor skills* enable her to perform actions involving large movements, such as throwing and catching.

- **cognitive and symbolic** Cognitive and symbolic development involves gaining knowledge and skills for processing and using information in a meaningful way. These skills include imagination and creativity, abstract thought, logical reasoning, problem-solving and determined action.
- **linguistic and symbolic** Learning to talk involves the ability to vocalise (or say words), comprehend and acquire an ever-expanding vocabulary. Children learn to use language in increasingly complex ways, for example by expressing opinions and exploring their thoughts.
- **emotional and social** From being a baby who is totally reliant on her carers, a child becomes increasingly independent. She develops self-help skills and an understanding of social and cultural perspectives. Control over the emotions develops together with an understanding of acceptable ways in which to demonstrate opinions and feelings.
- **moral and spiritual** Moral development broadly concerns understanding values such as honesty, fairness and respect, concepts such as right and wrong, responsibility and the consequences of one's actions. Spiritual development is a growth in the ability to perceive absolutes and their underlying effect on people and the world.

Each aspect of development is intricately linked and if one aspect is hampered or neglected in some way a child will fail to reach her full potential. It is the responsibility of the child's carers to ensure that all her needs are met. Play is as important for a child's developmental needs as good nutrition, warmth and protection. It provides opportunities to improve gross and fine motor skills and maintain physical health. It helps to develop imagination and creativity, provides a context in which to practise social skills, acts as an outlet for emotional expression and provides opportunities to understand value systems. Providing for play includes ensuring that the child has opportunities, resources and time for play appropriate to her stage of development (see Section 4).

DEVELOPMENTAL PROGRESS

Mary Sheridan identified broad stages of development through which children pass (see *From Birth to Five Years*). These recognisable stages provide a kind of map of development, which can be used to give an indication of a child's progress and to identify that child's individual needs.

The idea that play also develops sequentially was put forward by early theorists such as Friedrich von Schiller in the 1880s and Charlotte Buhler in the 1930s. Since then work has been carried out by researchers (including Mary Sheridan) to identify and describe each stage in the sequence.

As children develop so does their play. If you compare children of various ages, it is easy to see how different they are (see Section 2). Play may begin spontaneously as soon as interaction is established between a baby and another person or her immediate environment, for example smiling in response to an adult's attention, finding and playing with her toes or experimenting with making sounds. As primary reflexes diminish, the baby is free to start determining her actions and to engage in more and more elaborate forms of play. Therefore, play not only contributes to development by allowing children to learn, practise and perfect new skills, but also acts as an indicator of how their development is progressing.

The level of skill that children display in performing certain activities increases as they develop. For example, when observing a child of 6 years and a child of 3 years playing catch, it is noticeable that the older child will be more adept at catching the ball than the younger child (see Section 3).

TYPES OF PLAY

It is possible to identify distinct types of play which represent and contribute to progress in different areas of development. Theorists are divided over the best way to categorise elements of play. The categories chosen here best reflect Dr Sheridan's classifications. However, they have been extended to include current terms for types of play.

Active play

Active play is particularly important for physical development as it involves using head, trunk and limbs in sitting, crawling, standing, running, climbing, jumping, throwing, kicking and catching. It may also involve rough and tumble play and is a means of gaining strength, agility and co-ordination. Active play is seen in babies very early, in fact, as soon as they begin to control their head and limbs.

Explorative and manipulative play

Exploratory and manipulative play usually starts from about 3 months when babies engage in 'finger play'. This kind of play is important for sensory development, fine movements and hand–eye co-ordination. It involves the child in exploring her environment and finding out about the properties of objects through the senses (sight, sound, smell, touch and taste).

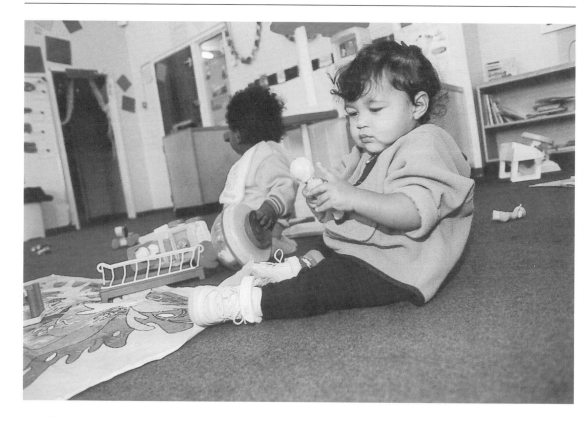

Exploratory and manipulative play contributes to the child's understanding of the permanence of objects and an appreciation of the implications of time and space.

Imitative play

Babies and children copy the actions they see repeatedly performed by others and this is an important feature of social and cognitive and symbolic development. Imitative play indicates that the child has observed an action and is able to recognise that it is repeated and therefore in some way significant. For example, after a visit to the library a child may pretend to be the librarian and recreate loaning books in her play. Imitative play begins very early on in momentary episodes. Even a very young baby might, for example, move her tongue in and out imitating an adult in close proximity to her.

Imitative play reflects what a child sees and hears going on around her, particularly in her everyday, social and cultural context. It is necessary in order for a child to learn the quickest and most effective way of performing meaningful actions for herself.

Constructive play

Constructive (or construction) play involves creating something such as a tower of building blocks. It requires a combination of fine movements, sensory capacity and cognitive and symbolic understanding. To build something a child needs not only to be able to manipulate the components, but also to be able to visualise and plan the object in her head.

Pretend play

Through observation and imitation children begin to invent make-believe situations for themselves. Role play can make best use of a minimum amount of resources. For example, a hat can immediately provide the child with a new role. Pretend play is an opportunity to put insights and skills into action and is therefore dependent on the use of imagination and creativity. There will be cultural variations of which early years workers should be aware.

Games with rules

Games with rules assume a degree of understanding about sharing, taking turns, fair play and the accurate recording of results. Games with rules usually start at about 4 years when small groups of children begin to improvise their own rules for co-operative play. Team games which challenge competitiveness in older children and adults become increasingly subject to rules.

PLAYING AND SOCIAL INTERACTION

Mildred Parten (working in the 1930s) and others have identified aspects of how children play in relation to other children. The following categories of social play are no longer thought of as a hierarchy of progression, but rather as descriptions of different kinds of social play which emerge from infancy through to early childhood.

- **solitary/solo play**   The child plays alone.
- **spectator play/'looking on' play**   The child is engaged in watching other children but not joining them.
- **parallel play**   The child plays alongside other children, but with fleeting interaction with them.
- **associative play**   The children may be engaged in associated activities in close proximity, but have their own ideas about their play.
- **co-operative play**   The children co-operate with each other over play, ideas and equipment for periods of their play.

THEORIES ABOUT PLAY

Many different theories about play exist. Theorists have struggled for centuries to describe and explain the universal significance of play without consensus. However, stretching from Greek philosophers such as Plato in the first century to Rousseau and Pestalozzi in the seventeenth century and Freud and Piaget in the nineteenth and twentieth centuries, it is possible to trace general agreement that play is not random or meaningless, but that it fulfils a distinct and important purpose. Theorists emphasise different aspects of play and it is this that distinguishes one theory from another.

THE CHILD AS AN ACTIVE LEARNER

Some theorists, such as Piaget and Bruner recognised that children are active in their learning or, in other words, learn by doing. Play often involves the child reconstructing an experience in her own way, drawing on her imagination and creativity, and also combining this with the social conventions that she has accepted. For example, a child might create a scenario with a group of toys in which one toy represents the mother and another toy represents the child. This is sometimes referred to as a social constructivist theory.

PSYCHO-DYNAMIC THEORIES

Some theorists see specific links between play and children's emotions. According to this school of thought, play is a means of expressing feelings, coming to terms with difficulties, reliving enjoyable experiences and gaining control over conflicting emotions. Freud is generally acknowledged to be the pioneer of psycho-dynamic theories which were extended and refined by such theorists as Erikson and later Winnicott.

Another psycho-dynamic thinker, Melanie Klein, put forward the theory that emotional conflicts and anxieties are revealed as a child plays. By observing children, she believed that it was possible to identify problems that could then be resolved by encouraging and guiding the child's play.

CHART OF THEORISTS

The following chart is arranged in alphabetical order for simplicity and is not in any order of priority. It provides a brief guide to some well-known theorists who have contributed to our present understanding of play. It is not intended to be an exhaustive list of theorists and the authors are not recommending that any one theory is more important than another.

Table 1.1 Chart of theorists		
Theorist	Dates	Key ideas
Chris Athey	Twentieth century	Developed the concept of *schemas* (a pattern of repeatable behaviour into which experiences are assimilated). Athey's theory has been influential in our observations of children and in planning curricula.
Jerome Bruner	1915–	Bruner believed that children need to be physically active and to have firsthand experiences to develop ideas and the ability to think. Play provides many such opportunities for this.
Erik H. Erikson	1902–1979	Erikson developed Freud's theories about personality and the mind. He was interested in the link between imaginative play and the emotions. His work also compared adults' play to that of children.
Friedrich Froebel	1782–1852	Froebel started the Kindergarten movement. His theories have remained at the heart of thinking about early years care and education. Froebel believed that children learn through active play and that their learning is most effective when they are engaged in imaginative and pretend play, which involves them in deep thought. He saw great value in outdoor activities which encourage free movement and involve the child in exploring the environment. He also favoured creative activities such as arts and crafts, music and books.

Table 1.1 Chart of theorists		
Theorist	Dates	Key ideas
Susan Issacs	1885–1948	Susan Issacs was influenced by the work of Froebel. She saw play as a means for children to express their feelings. She also believed that more formal learning should wait until around the age of seven.
Maria Montessori	1870–1952	Maria Montessori was a doctor who worked with children with learning disabilities. She concentrated on learning through structured rather than spontaneous play. Based on the idea that children are active learners, she developed a theory that they are more receptive to different types of learning at different stages in their early development. She did not believe that children were capable of creativity until they had worked through a series of structured learning activities.
Jean Piaget	1896–1980	Piaget is regarded as one of the major theorists in child development. His work on how thinking develops is based on the idea that a sequence of four stages can be identified. The stages are: • sensori-motor stage (birth to 18 months) • developing operations (18 months to 7 years) • concrete operations (7 to 12 years) • formal operations (12 years to adulthood)
Lev Vygotsky	1896–1934	Vygotsky believed that children benefit from play because it allows them to engage in activities from which they are excluded in reality, such as flying an aeroplane. His work also places great emphasis on the importance of the adult's role in enhancing the child's ideas and thinking.
D.W. Winnicott	1896–1974	Winnicott believed that play is essential to social and emotional development and that play and learning are very closely related. He particularly influenced our understanding of the important role of comforters (such as teddy bears) for children and called these *transitional objects*.

SUMMARY

- Play makes a vital contribution to every child's development.
- Play has different functions.
- Different types of play can be identified.
- There are many different theories about play.

Most of the drawings that follow are based on photographs. The approximate ages of the children at the time the pictures were taken are included underneath the illustrations. *These are not necessarily the earliest or latest ages at which the particular play behaviour appears.*

Ages and stages in the development of play

This section describes in detail how children's play develops from birth to 6 years, based on the sequence of stages identified by Mary Sheridan. Making observations with a knowledge of identifiable developmental stages helps to focus the planning and provision of appropriate play activities. However, while these stages provide useful indicators, they should not be viewed rigidly. Global research studies have shown that there is a great deal of variance in the way that children's play develops. It is important to remember that children are individuals who develop at different rates. A great many social and cultural factors contribute to the variations. In a book of this length it is not possible to cover these factors or the numerous intermediate phases and transitions. However, a bibliography has been included which provides further sources of in-depth reading.

0–12 MONTHS

The baby's main carers have a crucial role to play not only in ensuring that the child's basic needs are met, but also in providing stimulation for her developing senses. The vigorous movements, the smiles and the 'coos' that young babies make when handled and talked to by their parents or carers are clear responses to enjoyable stimulation. They quickly learn to attract the attention of their carers and this coupled with the lively interactions that follow can be seen as the very early stages of play.

6 weeks. When she is picked up and talked to by a familiar carer, a lively interchange takes place involving simultaneous looking, listening, vocalising and bodily movements.

12 weeks. Lying on her front, lifting her head and resting on her forearms she scratches at the surface on which she lies, apparently enjoying the simultaneous sight and sound of her finger movements.

12 weeks. She grasps a rattle (or toy) firmly, but is still unable to co-ordinate holding the toy with visual attention.

While newborns are able to move their limbs, their movements are initially uncontrolled and influenced by inborn reflexes (Landsdowne and Walker 1991: 73). These reflexes gradually fade as the baby's physical (gross and fine movements) and sensory (sight and sound recognition, etc.) abilities develop.

As babies mature they start to engage in play activities which are purposefully directed and visually controlled, such as reaching for toys. Hand/eye co-ordination is demonstrated at about 10 to 12 weeks. Lying on her back with her head in the midline, a baby will deliberately bring her hands together over her upper chest, converge her eyes on her hands and engage in active interlacing finger play.

At about the same age, when lying on her tummy, holding her head and shoulders up steadily, she will open and shut her hands and scratch at the surface on which she is lying. She appears to be interested and enjoys the simultaneous sight and sensation of her moving fingers and the sound this produces.

Given a toy such as a rattle to hold, she will grasp it firmly and bring it towards her face sometimes bashing her chin. Usually any glances she makes at the object are fleeting. At this age she finds it difficult to control her head, neck and eye muscles and keep her hand in a 'static' grasp at the same time.

By about 14 weeks she can hold a toy and look at it steadily. At about 18–20 weeks she can reach for and grasp a toy which is offered and look at it for a longer length of time. She will shake it and also take it to her mouth and away again. She holds the toy between her two hands, clasping and unclasping it alternately. She can drop the toy by opening both hands wide, but cannot yet place it down deliberately. By about 5 ½ months she has discovered her feet.

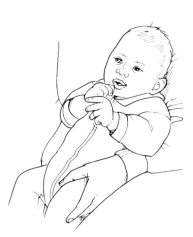

12 weeks. With head and back well supported, she demonstrates good hand/eye co-ordination in finger play.

18 weeks. As consistent hand/eye co-ordination is achieved, she holds the toy between her hands, opening and closing them alternately.

5 ½ months. She brings her extended legs into a vertical position and reaches out in foot/eye co-ordination.

About 6–9 months

6 months. With a concentrated expression she takes a characteristic age-related, two-handed approach to a block. (Immediately after this she took it to her mouth.)

By 6 months she has increasing control of her movements and hand/eye co-ordination enabling her to reach out for and take hold of toys within reach of her extended arms. She often uses her feet to help her clasp a toy or bring objects to her mouth. She is still unable to release toys voluntarily from her grasp. When a toy falls from her hand and it is outside her range of vision, it appears that it has ceased to exist for her.

Between 6 and 7 months she begins to appreciate the 'two-ness' of hands and a week or two later, of feet. This means that she can hold two objects simultaneously, one in each hand, using a firm palmar grasp and bring her hands together to match them. She can now pass a toy from one hand to the other, releasing the toy from her hand at will.

At about 7 months she clearly demonstrates the ability to tell the difference between familiar people and strangers. Around 8–9 months she sits steadily on the floor stretching out in all directions for toys within her reach and without falling over. She begins to crawl and reach towards eye-catching objects that are out of range.

6 months. Having grasped the toy with both hands, she transferred it to her right hand and brought the toy to her mouth.

9 months. She sits on the floor and can reach sideways.

At this age she is showing some awareness of the permanence of objects. (Previously objects out of her view ceased to exist for her.) For example, she can now lift a cushion to look underneath it for a toy which she has observed being partly hidden. Two or three weeks later she can do the same with an object that she has watched being completely hidden.

She can lean over the side of her buggy or chair to watch a falling toy and keep it in view. She can even begin to throw toys about for the satisfaction of throwing and also the sight and sound of what happens when an object falls, perhaps rolls away and then comes to a standstill. She enjoys both the sensation and noise she can produce by banging and sliding toys across hard surfaces.

Around this time she seems to look carefully at a new toy as if judging its qualities before reaching for it. She prefers to concentrate on one toy at a time, manipulating it carefully. A little later she can use two objects in combination, such as banging two toys together. This may be imitating an action performed by somebody else or the result of a discovery that she has made for herself.

As babies become more mobile they tend to keep close to their mother or main carer, partly for reassurance and partly to seek attention and co-operation in play. Babies show recognition of the familiar voices of their carers very early on. By around 9–12 months a baby will clearly show that she is beginning to understand short phrases and simple instructions given to her and repeated by those with whom she is familiar. She likes to watch and listen to familiar adults and children doing day-to-day activities and enjoys being part of this social interaction. All-round early learning depends on the quality and quan-
tity of affectionate one-to-one

About 9–12 months

9 months. Poking at small objects with one index finger is characteristic for this age, so too is the 'mirror' posture of the other hand.

10 months. She enjoys the sight and sound of banging toys.

11 months. She moves along carrying two objects at the same time.

11 months. She will take her first steps with encouragement.

12 months. Holding on to the furniture, she moves around and investigates objects of interest – particularly parcels and receptacles.

attention and encouragement towards independence that the baby receives from her carers.

At this stage the baby's attention is mainly satisfied by her perceptions of things here and now. However, immediate, brief imitations that she performs show that her short-term memory is developing. Long-term memory develops as her perceptions and experiences are stored away. These are then retrievable as she shows recognition and starts to assemble memories into more complex and creative patterns of thought.

During their first year of life, babies gain increasing competence in their ability to interact with their environment. They show an intense curiosity and desire to explore. They find that being able to move about enables them to gain a working knowledge of the nature and possibilities of their world. They also learn that their wishes, attitudes and intentions can be communicated and they begin to do so in increasingly sophisticated ways.

12 months. She cannot yet name these objects, but she can demonstrate their use.

12 months. He has thrown out all his playthings and calls loudly for their return. This demonstrated the child's understanding of the permanence of objects.

12 months. She grasps the crayon in an age-appropriate fashion. A few moments later she shifted the crayon to the other hand.

During this period, children become increasingly mobile and inquisitive. Their world of attention is rapidly expanding and they want to take a closer look at and have a more active part in what is happening. By imitating and repeating activities that they see performed, they clearly display their dawning recognition of cause and effect.

From this stage a child will start demonstrating more obvious and prolonged 'definition-by-use' in relation to common objects, such as drinking from an empty cup or bringing a comb to her hair. At first, these activities are simple and very brief. However, they soon become more complex, last longer, are sequentially correct and directed towards some purposeful activity.

She can manipulate toys with a good pincer grasp. She rarely places more than two or three objects together in a line or tower. She enjoys multi-sensory experiences, such as the sight, sound and feel of tearing paper. Increasing skill in walking and moving around enables her to push and pull large wheeled toys and guide smaller ones by hand. She transports her collection of toys and other suitable objects from one place to another, varying the weight and size of the loads.

She has an overwhelming desire to explore and enjoys discovering how to put objects in and out of containers. She peers into toy boxes to manipulate, smell and taste the toys within. Sometimes she will show the toys that she has found to her carer. She may attempt to make some show of replacing the toys in the box, but scatters them around. She will discard toys indiscriminately, perhaps dropping or throwing them when they cease to be of interest to her.

ABOUT 12–18 MONTHS

12 months. This give-and-take play involved the taking of turns in exchanging toys and conversation.

13 months. This partially sighted baby shows give-and-take play in response to spoken invitation.

12 months. *He enjoys sharing a book and at the same time has not forgotten the two spoons he holds.*

Her interests are still largely focused on familiar carers and surroundings. She greatly enjoys the active use of safe, familiar household objects, such as pots and pans and begins to take part in short episodes of role play.

She communicates her needs and feelings effectively, using a combination of expressive gestures, loud, tuneful voice sounds and a small but ever-increasing range of single words. She may also show a growing interest in naming objects in pictures, repeating words, and watching and listening to people talk.

One toy or comforter object, such as a blanket may have particular significance and is carried everywhere. She will be distressed if the comforter is taken away from her and will fret if it is lost or unavailable.

At this stage she is only able to deal with her own needs and is unable to consider the needs of other children, siblings or animals. This is known as the *egocentric stage*. As she begins to make the distinction between 'me' and 'not me' she will begin to move away from the unshakeable belief that all things rightly belong to her, towards an appreciation of what is 'mine' and 'not mine' and of what is 'yours' and 'theirs'.

14 months. *He enjoys putting objects in and out of containers.*

15 months. *Around this age he understands the function of a brush and comb and is now able to use a recognisable version of the word.*

15 months. *He squats on the floor looking at a picture book and turns several pages at a time.*

Rapidly improving control of the body and limbs allows the child to engage in activities such as pushing, pulling and carrying large objects. For example, sitting on a small tricycle she can steer it well, but propels it forward with her feet on the ground.

She explores endlessly and because her sense of danger is very limited she needs constant supervision. She is becoming increasingly interested in examining small objects – looking for minute detail. She will open boxes and drawers, rummage among the contents, throw some objects away, pull others to pieces, tear off wrappers, bang, hammer and poke.

She will play contentedly with suitable toys, for example building blocks, simple puzzles and soft toys for long periods, providing she knows that a familiar and attentive adult is nearby. She continues to enjoy putting small toys in and out of containers. Once she has discovered (or been given the idea), she builds towers varying from about three blocks at 18 months to six or more blocks at 2 years. Materials such as clay, dough, water and sand provide her with opportunities to experiment.

Her drawings display bold, widespread brushwork demonstrating the increasing co-ordination of hand and eye. She holds pencils and paintbrushes in the middle or towards the top of the shaft using the whole hand. With the pencil or brush held between thumb and fingers she draws spontaneous to and fro marks. She may begin to show preference for one hand, but continues to use either hand or sometimes both hands at the same time.

In the early role play and pretend play that is characteristic of

18–24 MONTHS

18 months. The discovery of control over a push-and-pull toy is clearly demonstrated here.

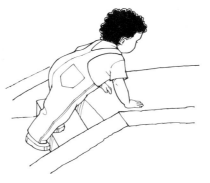

18 months. A few weeks older, he can now walk backwards and sideways, pulling and steering a toy containing a collection of bricks.

19 months. Crawling swiftly up the garden steps, this child demonstrates the usual sequence of movements – right hand, left foot, left hand, right foot.

20 months. *She enjoys the simultaneous sight, sound and muscular precision of her hammering activity.*

24 months. *She is using readily available boots for her role play.*

this stage, she will use materials that are near to hand, but often in a fleeting way. For example, pretending to put herself to bed for a few moments, she lies down, closes her eyes and pulls a cover over herself, but only if coverings are available. Other examples are going through the movements of driving a car, usually making suitable engine noises if she has a seat and a steering wheel of sorts or pretending to read a book if one is there.

She puts two or three toys together meaningfully (for example, a doll on a chair or bricks in a truck), but soon she will start making one object represent another and miming to symbolise things that are not there.

By 18 months a child will usually speak using between 6 and 20 recognisable single words, such as 'tup' (cup), 'dink' (drink), 'baw' (ball), 'loo' (look), 'der' (there), 'uh' (up), 'dow' (down). She is able to use these words in the appropriate context and might also use some meaningful utterances (holophrases), which to her are single words such as 'gimme' (give me), 'hee–ya' (here you are), 'awgone' (all gone) and 'do–way' (go away). She will use intonation appropriately and understands a great many more words than she uses. At about 21 months she begins to put two or more words together to frame short sentences. These sentences usually concern immediate issues for the child. She combines finger pointing, hand pulling and urgent vocalisation with a few words and phrases thrown in. She is able to understand most of what is said to her if simple language is used.

Children begin to demonstrate their understanding that minia-

24 months. *This boy is engaging in imitative role play developing into inventive imaginative play.*

2 ¼ years. *This child with special needs is involved in pretend play.*

ture toys represent objects and people in the real world. They begin to arrange such toys in meaningful groups that represent their use in everyday situations.

At this stage children appear confused about the size of toys in relation to themselves. For example, they will try to sit on a miniature chair, ride a miniature horse or step into a miniature vehicle. A little later, when they have realised these impossibilities, they may still attempt to place large soft toys in containers that are too small.

Constant sympathetic adult encouragement helps the child engage in spontaneous play. This adult encouragement aids cognitive and symbolic development in children between 1 and 2 years of age. However, it is still difficult for a child to see things from another person's perspective.

Through grasping, banging, poking, throwing, holding, carrying and manipulating objects and finally incorporating these skills into imaginative play, a child makes many important discoveries. First, she discovers through seeing and feeling the particular properties of objects. She then learns what she can do with the objects and their particular functions and finally she learns how to adapt them to her own requirements. In other words, she discovers their potential.

Around this time she will follow a simple story, read aloud, look at the pictures and enjoy the close proximity of a familiar adult that this activity brings. This interest in books, words and pictures is important in language development and soon she will begin to make comments and ask questions.

1 ½, 2 and 2 ½ years. These children are enjoying musical sounds in solo play in close proximity.

2 ½ years. A boy with profound hearing loss playing with his teacher's radio.

20 months. Like all children of this age, she has an irresistible urge to get in and out of large boxes perhaps learning her own relative size and position.

4 years. This boy with learning difficulties is discovering the relationship between his size and shape, and the inside volume of a large cardboard box.

2 AND 3 YEARS

Two to three-year-olds enjoy toys such as balls, large construction play, matching and sorting games, threading toys, trucks to pull and push, sand and water play, simple computer games, musical instruments and books.

From the age of 2 a child shows increasing skill in both gross and fine movements. She lifts, carries, climbs, leaps and runs. She can sit on a small tricycle and manoeuvre it with her feet, pedalling and steering round corners. She may attempt to kick a ball, but usually walks into it. She can throw a ball without falling over, but her attempts to catch it are not yet successful.

Her manipulative and constructive skills show steady improvement. She builds a tower of six or seven bricks at 2 years progressing to nine or ten bricks at 3 years. Her preferred hand is used for most activities and when she picks up a pencil or crayon she usually uses her thumb and two fingers well down the shaft towards the point. This increasing control enables her to experiment with circular scribbles as well as to and fro strokes. Brushwork is bold and covers large areas. She enjoys simple colourful inset jigsaw puzzles. By 3 years of age she can match two or three primary colours and shapes.

Children of this age use a lively form of communication expressing themselves through words, gestures and mime – either separately or in combination. Developments in language are immediately reflected in children's play.

2 ½ years. With increasingly fine motor skill, threading beads is a fascinating activity.

2 ½ years. While painting at the table, he is indifferent to the fact that the pictures are upside down.

A child will still tend to follow familiar adults around enjoying imitation, calling attention to her efforts, seeking approval and by 3 years she may start to ask questions, such as 'what?', 'where?' and 'who?'. Her earlier role play is now extended as she becomes more imaginative. During this imaginative play she talks aloud to herself giving a running commentary on her actions and instructing herself. Later she uses vocabulary more closely linked to the activity. She demonstrates that she is beginning to use forward planning, for example, by collecting suitable items for going on a pretend journey.

Playing at this stage comprises a combination of solo play, 'looking on' play and associative play as she begins to interact with other children. Their ability to communicate is limited and they have difficulty understanding the need to share adult attention and toys.

Between 2 and 3 years, the child seems convinced that a familiar adult automatically understands what she sees, feels, needs and intends. For example, a child looking out of an upstairs window would assume that a familiar adult downstairs can see what she sees from upstairs. She is still unable to see things from another person's perspective, but with experience she will begin to understand other viewpoints.

3 years. *She enjoys the appearance and behaviour of bubbles.*

3 years. *This child with learning disabilities is looking with interest at a book.*

2 ½ and 3 years. *Water play provides opportunities for solo play in close proximity. Each child has their own play things and play space.*

3 years. *This child with special needs is bathing her doll.*

3 AND 4 YEARS

At around the age of 3, children begin to interact with other children more readily – usually in a small group situation closely attached to one or two familiar adults. During the next year they make rapid strides in socialisation, which broadens their circle of friends. Their demand for constant attention from familiar adults decreases, because they are secure in the knowledge that it is available when needed.

At this stage children favour outdoor, construction play, indoor table and floor games, and socio-dramatic play. This is usually elaborated and carried on from day-to-day, and is characterised by an ever-increasing understanding of the need for discussion, planning, sharing, taking turns and playing by agreed rules.

From 3 years there is growing control over limbs and movement. A child of this age runs with more confidence, can walk backwards and sideways and balance on one foot. She often climbs stairs one foot to a step and descends stairs two feet to a step. She enjoys jumping a short distance without falling over and rides a tricycle with confidence using the pedals and steering safely around corners. Her spatial awareness is well developed and she can manoeuvre herself and her toys around objects.

Construction play involves carrying large blocks, planks and boards to make houses, spaceships, cars, hospitals, shops and other structures to carry out many imaginative activities, which often involve other children.

3 years. This boy is engaged in imaginative play.

4 ½ years. This boy with autism is playing with a small chime of bells.

Fine motor skills are also rapidly improving through play with blocks, simple craft activities, for example, involving the use of scissors and beads, small world play, musical instruments, wood-work and simple computer activities. From 3 years onwards more complex jigsaw puzzles are needed and it is interesting to note that children of this age may be more interested in fitting the pieces together rather than building up the whole picture.

Play with malleable materials, such as dough, continues to be an absorbing activity. Spontaneous drawings become increasingly elaborate and diverse in colour, form and content and generally concern people, houses, transport vehicles, flowers, animals, etc. While she paints, the child may provide a running commentary and change her mind about what the painting represents as she goes along. It is not until about 4 years that she announces beforehand what she is about to draw, indicating that she has some idea in mind of what the picture will look like before she begins. There are clear signs that she is beginning to control her attention, choosing to stop an activity and return to it later.

Music making can be an inexpensive and enjoyable activity, using the voice with simple or home-made instruments, which serves to encourage rhythm, pitch and the ability to distinguish different sounds. Some children may show exceptional talent and ability at an early age.

3 years. This girl is reversing a tricycle into a small space.

3 ¾ years. This partially sighted boy is playing with miniature toys. He has grouped all these items within his visual field.

At 3 years, although she possesses a large vocabulary, her sentence structure and her pronunciation may still be immature. She is beginning to use language in a variety of ways, for example, taking turns in conversation, talking about things, making requests and giving instructions. She may be able to give an account of past events. A combination of words, gestures and facial expressions is understood by her peers.

3 ½ and 3 years. These children are making models.

3 ½ years. This child with hearing and visual difficulties enjoys playing with small world toys. Note anticipatory posture of right hand.

4 years. Handed a box of miniature cars, she scrutinises the collection in its original place, before selecting items for assembly. A younger child would probably first spread them all out on the table top.

By 4 years, she can give an informative account of a recent experience and uses a variety of questions, such as 'Can I have?', 'When?' and 'Why?'. She can also be argumentative, and absurdities in language make her laugh. Four-year-olds have a broad sense of humour and delight in rhymes, riddles, simple jokes and verbal teasing. They enjoy having stories read to them especially when they can see illustrations at the same time.

The child at this age is able to use positional words such as 'in', 'behind' and 'under'. Some pronunciations are difficult, such as, 'th' and 'r'. Her grammar is usually correct and she tries to make grammatically irregular words fit grammatical rules, for example 'I drived it'.

Children may act out puppet shows and appropriate television programmes they have seen. When playing in a group, they assign each other roles. Often one child makes most of the decisions about who plays which roles. With negotiation these roles may be alternated.

At this stage a child's imaginative, subjective world is so vivid that she is sometimes hazy concerning what is fact and what is fiction. An inexperienced early years worker may be startled by a child's apparent blatant disregard for objective truth!

Involvement in imaginative play helps her cope with strong emotions. She may show sensitivity to the needs of others especially if they are hurt. At this age children often show great fondness for family pets and often include them in imaginative activities.

Around this age she will be fascinated by cause and effect. Exploration and curiosity about the environment are not always matched by an appreciation of its dangers and adult supervision is necessary.

3 ½ and 5 years. These children are involved in an elaborate imaginative game.

11 years. This child has severe learning difficulties and is playing happily with the sand tray.

5 AND 6 YEARS

From this stage onwards a child steadily continues to develop her everyday competence and powers of communication. In her play she shows increasing enjoyment, not only of elaborate imaginative activities, but also of complex indoor and outdoor games.

Around this age children begin to participate in team games and games with rules. They may begin to show a particular aptitude or preference for sporting, craft or creative activities. For the next few years distinctions may emerge between the spontaneous play of boys and girls. Therefore, it is important that early years workers provide equal opportunities for all children to participate in all activities.

2 years, 5 years and 8 years. These children of different ages are talking and sharing a book together.

5 years. This early years worker is reinforcing communication by eye and hand contact with a child who has little or no spoken language.

5 and 6 years. These children are enjoying climbing apparatus.

There is significant progress in agility and strength at this age. A child can jump and kick a ball several metres and is capable of learning to ride a two-wheeled bike with stabilisers.

Drawing becomes more sophisticated with increasing pencil/brush control and her grasp is similar to that of an adult. She enjoys talking, telling and making up jokes often using longer sentences. She understands the need for taking turns in conversation.

Her spontaneous play activities are beginning to confirm her scientific understanding of concepts such as measurement. Role play may become quite detailed as children decide roles in advance and plan how the role play will progress. She is able to consider the needs of others, showing that she is able to 'decentre' and may start to help and guide younger children in their play. Increasingly she distinguishes between fact and fantasy.

6 years. She shows skills of agility and strength.

5 years. This child shows proficiency in skipping.

5 years. Child on a slide giving appropriate verbal instruction to her doll.

This section provides examples of particular play sequences involving certain activities. The illustrations show the identifiable stages of development in how children typically investigate, manipulate and use play objects. All children do appear to pass through broad stages of development in their spontaneous play. However, this is dependent on appropriate opportunities being available to them, adult support and encouragement, and cultural practices. The ages selected are used as examples and in reality often vary.

Outlines of

some

significant

play

sequences

CUP PLAY

6 months. Having grasped the cup with both hands, she passes it to one hand and brings the most prominent feature of the cup to her mouth.

9 months. Grasping the cup the right way up with both hands, he brings the rim to his mouth while looking at his carer.

12 months. Having just observed the carer stroking the rim of this cup, she seizes the cup and spoon and successfully imitates the action.

12 months. She is now reminded of the true function of cups and spoons, which shows a clear example of definition-by-use.

2 ¼ years. Cups, spoons and other items are incorporated into pretend play.

BLOCK PLAY

12 months. Having found a block hidden under the cup, she begins to explore some further possibilities on her own.

9 months. She is holding a block competently in each hand, interested in comparing them, she brings them together. A few moments later she found considerable pleasure in clicking them together.

15 months. She still enjoys handling blocks and readily builds small towers of two or three blocks with her right hand while grasping a larger soft toy with her left hand.

3 years. Before it was possible to provide a model bridge, she used up every block in sight and is counting them aloud. This is an example of previous learning.

2 years. Having built half the tower with his right hand, he shifted attention to his left hand, indicating that he is learning independently.

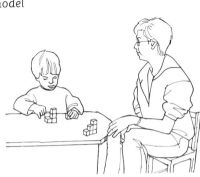

3 ½ years. He has much experience of construction block play and has no difficulty in copying the model constructed by the adult.

BALL PLAY

18 months. He is still too uncertain of his legs to stand on one foot. He walks into a large ball, but is unable to kick it.

2 years. Although still unable to kick the ball, she steadily raises her arms to balance, lifts her foot momentarily but without the desired result.

3 years. She is able to kick a large ball gently, but cannot yet co-ordinate her eyes, arms and hands to catch a ball.

4 years. This child with learning disabilities is making a positive attempt to co-ordinate movements of eyes and limbs in order to catch a large ball.

3 ½ years. With greater capability, his head, body posture and the position of his legs, arms and hands are held in anticipation.

3 ½ years. She has yet to develop the skills needed for catching a smaller ball approaching at speed.

3 ½ years. He engages his whole body in throwing a ball at the skittles.

4 ½ years. She employs a running approach to kick the ball with total attention.

4 ½ years. This boy is throwing a small ball; his eyes focused on the target.

DRAWING AND PAINTING

15 months. He shows a palmar grasp of the pencil lower down the shaft and makes to and fro lines and dots. Notice again how his left hand mirrors the posture of his right hand.

21 months. She is using her whole arm to produce large brush strokes as she paints at an easel.

12 months. This girl is using a typical grasp of a pencil at its proximal end with her right hand (notice how her left hand mirrors the posture of her right hand). A moment later she passed the pencil from right to left again making marks on the paper.

3 ½ years. She grips the pencil with her right hand and attempts to copy strokes. She does not engage her left hand.

3 ½ years. He is showing an example of simultaneous two-handed performance. The pencil grip is now near the tip of the pencil.

4 years. The right hand shows a mature grip of the pencil while her left hand steadies the paper. Her drawing is clearly recognisable as a house.

7 years. This boy with autism has good vision and hearing. He has spent a long time on the details of his painting, which his carers will need his help in interpreting.

3 ½ and 4 years. These children are beginning to make good representations of the human figure with increasing detail.

4 ¾ years. She has been drawing and colouring with intense concentration and is beginning to include surrounding features, such as a yellow sun.

SMALL WORLD PLAY

21 months. This child had just been given a boxed model town. He named the houses, flats and trees but did not group them, preferring to treat the items rather like an inset jigsaw puzzle.

3 years. Using the same boxed model town, this 3-year-old lined up all the houses and flats in one neat row and the cars in another row, telling himself aloud who lived in each house and flat.

5 years. Using the same model town, this 5-year-old chose the positioning of the houses, flats and railway carefully. She decided that the railway should be behind the houses and that the houses and flats should have space around them. The cars were placed at the station awaiting the return of the commuters.

6 ½ years. This 6 ½-year-old arranged the same model town in a realistic fashion. Her younger sister is engaged in her own play, insisting on the inclusion of her jumbo-jet, which the elder sister allowed to land in a nearby field.

This section covers:

- the role of adults in spontaneous play
- providing for play
- safety issues
- managing a child centred environment
- observation and assessment
- play and the developing sense of self
- promoting equal opportunities
- why usual patterns of play development may change

Providing for play: the role of adults

THE ROLE OF ADULTS IN SPONTANEOUS PLAY

The adult's role is central in enabling and empowering children in their play. It is essential that all early years workers understand and value spontaneous play in order to become sensitive facilitators. While most children embark on spontaneous play willingly as active participants, adults need to make the right provisions. It is important to remember that every child is an individual with her own needs and that during the process of development these needs will change.

PROVIDING FOR PLAY

Facilitating spontaneous play requires careful planning, anticipating the next stage and adapting resources to fulfil the particular needs of a child. In providing for play, adults should consider:

- space
- resources
- time
- friends

Space

Appropriate space should be set aside for play. It should be big enough to allow for the free-ranging activities of a child in relation to her age and developmental progress. Play space should be safe and should also lend itself to exploration and investigation by the child.

Resources

It is important to provide stimulating resources that are appropriate to the child's age and stage of development. Resources should be easily obtainable by the child. (Children who for instance are restricted by a physical disability will need to have toys placed within easy reach.) Early years workers should also ensure that resources are representative of a multi-cultural society. All play objects should be checked for safety.

Time

Spontaneous play depends on the child being given the opportunity to engage in activities without interruption. Children should be given enough time to fulfil whatever engages their interest.

Friends

At all stages of development children need playmates. Initially a baby needs the participation of her adult carers, but as she grows older and her communication and social skills increase, it is important for her to be able to interact with children of a similar age and stage. Enthusiasm and encouragement from adults should be available to children whenever they need it. Adults also have a crucial role in ensuring that the play environment is free from bullying and intimidation.

GOOD PROFESSIONAL PRACTICE

- The presence of a caring, responsible adult is essential in all play situations to maintain safety.
- Adults tend to be more interested in the product rather than the process of play. It is important to allow the child to gain satisfaction from the process rather than the end result. The 'doing' is the spontaneous play!
- The adult needs to have a clear understanding of when it is appropriate to intervene in children's play and when it is appropriate to stand back and observe unobtrusively.
- Early years workers should ensure that they review their expectations of spontaneous play regularly.

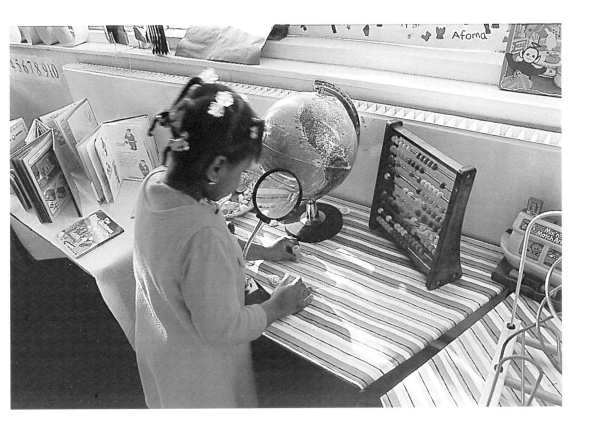

SAFETY ISSUES

Constant unobtrusive supervision of children engaged in spontaneous play is essential at all times. The nature of spontaneous play means that the adult needs to be particularly vigilant in respect to all aspects of safety concerning the child's choice and use of play equipment. Clear and current safety guidelines for early years workers and other adults need to be in place. As far as possible, children should understand these rules of safety.

MANAGING A CHILD CENTRED ENVIRONMENT

In a child centred environment, the child is the focus of all activities. Play is usually initiated by the child and taken further by the early years worker. Adults can facilitate child centred play by:

- taking children's play seriously
- being excited about their discoveries
- praising their achievements
- being patient and encouraging
- valuing the process of their play
- not always expecting a predictable end product

OBSERVATION AND ASSESSMENT

Observations are integral to a child centred approach to play, as they provide crucial information about a child's developmental and specific play needs. The value of carefully planned observation and assessment cannot be overemphasised. Observations can be used to:

- assess the child's individual needs for play
- assess the adequacy of the play resources already provided
- assess the adequacy of multi-cultural resources
- identify further resources
- identify any specialist help that may be required
- evaluate the role of the adult

It is important to know how to observe in order to collect the necessary data in the most useful, accurate and efficient way. Once the data has been collected, the early years worker needs to be able to evaluate it and make appropriate recommendations based on the findings. (For in-depth information on how to observe and assess see *How to Make Observations and Assessments* by J. Harding and L. Meldon-Smith (1996).)

Supervision and guidance from an experienced child care professional is helpful and can ensure that early years workers do not make assumptions about a child's expected stage of development.

Young children develop a sense of self, which is influenced by their environment and the response of others to them as individuals. A child with a poor self-image may make slower developmental progress. For example, a child whose first response is not to try a new play activity through fear of failure needs positive reinforcement of their self-image.

Fostering a positive self-image is particularly important with children who may be seen to differ from other children. This sense of difference may be the result of the child having a disability, needing to wear a sensory aid or being in the minority as part of a particular ethnic group. All adults involved in the care of children should be aware of the negative effects that feeling or being treated as different can have on a child's self-esteem and confidence. In all instances adults can help children develop a positive self-image through their careful use of language and handling of situations. A culture of inclusion which ensures that play resources are made available and accessible to all children will provide opportunities for all children to engage in and share the benefits of spontaneous play.

PLAY AND THE DEVELOPING SENSE OF SELF

Workers who observe and assess children regularly are more likely to be aware of children who choose from a limited range of play materials. Some children may be constrained in their choice of play by opinions they have internalised regarding the nature of 'boys' play activities' and 'girls' play activities'.

Early years workers should be guided in implementing clear equal opportunity policies. These policies need to be reviewed and updated on a regular basis.

Working in partnership with parents and carers is a crucial element of early years work. This involves being clear about the relative values that parents and carers attach to play. It also involves being clear about having a sensitive understanding of different cultural perspectives on the importance of play. This knowledge, coupled with good communication skills, can form the basis for positive discussions with parents and carers about the value of play-based learning and its importance for holistic development. Involving parents can be invaluable in providing for play. For example, their advice should be sought on appropriate clothing for role play.

PROMOTING EQUAL OPPORTUNITIES

WHY USUAL PATTERNS OF PLAY DEVELOPMENT MAY CHANGE

A variety of circumstances can occur in a child's life which may reduce or extinguish the motivation to play. These may include:

- illness
- poor nutrition
- traumatic events, such as bereavement or abuse
- having or developing special needs

Children with varying degrees of learning difficulties will possess the seeds of curiosity and motivation to play. With these children the adult may need to be the motivator and take a more active role in helping them to develop their play.

It is the responsibility of the early years worker to observe and assess all children individually. This provides information about the child's play and how to anticipate the next stage. Children who are experiencing difficulties need additional help in order to facilitate spontaneous play.

Organisations that support play

British Association for Early Childhood Education (Early Education), 111 City View House, 463 Bethnal Green Road, London E2 9QY

The association promotes the right of all children to education of the highest quality. It provides a multi-disciplinary network of support and advice for everyone concerned with the education and care of young children from birth to eight years.

National Children's Bureau, 8 Wakeley Street, London EC1V 7QE

The National Children's Bureau works to identify and promote the well-being and interests of all children and young people. It collects and disseminates information about children and promotes good practice in children's services through research, policy and practice development, membership, publications, conferences, training and an extensive library and information service.

National Play Information Centre, 199 Knightsbridge Road, London SW7 1DE

The National Play Information Centre is a large reference library and information service on children's play.

National Playbus Association, 93 Whitby Road, Bristol BS4 3QF

The National Playbus Association provides support, advice and information which helps keep playbuses on the road.

Pre-School Learning Alliance, 69 Kings Cross Road, London WC1X 9LL

The Pre-School Learning Alliance is a national educational charity with nearly 40 years' experience in the field of pre-school care and education in England. The membership consists of approximately 18,000 pre-schools attended by an estimated 850,000 children.

National Association of Toy and Leisure Libraries, 68 Church Way, London NW1 1LT

The National Association of Toy and Leisure Libraries promotes play and recreation by providing support for toy and leisure libraries, advice about appropriate toys and resources, information about starting and running a toy or leisure library, a range of publications on play (in relation to child development), and training for members and other people in the child care and disability fields. The association regrets that it is unable to answer queries from students.

Bibliography

Athey, C. (1990) *Extending Thought in Young Children: A Parent–Teacher Partnership*, London: Paul Chapman Publishing.

Bee, H. (1992) *The Developing Child*, New York: HarperCollins.

Bruce, T. (1996) *Helping Children to Play*, London: Hodder & Stoughton.

Bruce, T. and Meggitt, C. (1997) *Child Care and Education*, London: Hodder & Stoughton.

Bruner, J. (1990) *Acts of meaning*, Cambridge, MA: Harvard University Press.

Cass, J. (1977) *The Significance of Children's Play*, London: B.T. Batsford Ltd.

Chomsky, N. (1968) *Language and the Mind*, New York: Harcourt, Brace and World.

Davenport, G.C. (1989) *An Introduction to Child Development*, London: Unwin Hyman.

Donaldson, M. (1978) *Children's Minds*, London: Fortuna/Collins.

Drummand, M.J. (1993) *Assessing Children's Learning*, London: David Fulton.

Dunn, J. (1988) *The Beginnings of Social Understanding*, Oxford: Blackwell.

Elfer, P. 'Building intimacy in relationships with young children in nurseries' in *Early Years TACTYC Journal*, Spring 1996.

Geraghty, P. (1988) *Caring for Children*, 2nd edn, London: Balliere Tindall.

Harding, J. and Meldon-Smith, L. (1996) *How to Make Observations and Assessments*, Tyne and Wear: Hodder & Stoughton.

Hobart, C. and Frankel, J. (1995) *A Practical Guide to Activities for Young Children*, Cheltenham: Stanley Thornes.

Landsdowne, R. and Walker, M. (1991) *Your Child's Development from Birth to Adolesence*, London: Francis Lincoln.

Lindon, J. (1994) *Child Development from Birth to Eight: A Practical Focus*, Derby: National Children's Bureau.

Matterson, E.M. (1989) *Play with Purpose for the Under Sevens*, Harmondsworth: Penguin.

Middleton, L. (1992) *Children First-Working with Children and Disability*, Birmingham: Venture Press.

Petrie, P. (1987) *Baby Play*, London: Pantheon.

Piaget, J. (1962) *Play, Dreams and Imitation in Childhood*, London: Routledge & Kegan Paul.

Pugh, G. (ed.) (1992) *Contemporary Issues in Early Years: Working Collaboratively for Children*, London: Paul Chapman Publishing.

Swain, J. (ed.) (1993) *Disabling Barriers, Enabling Environments*, London: Sage Publications.

Sylva, K. and Lunt, I. (1988) *Child Development: A First Course*, Oxford: Blackwell.

Thomson, H. and Meggitt, C. (1987) *Human Growth and Development*, Tyne and Wear: Hodder & Stoughton.

Whalley, M. (1994) *Learning to be Strong: Integrating Education and Care in Early Childhood*, London: Hodder & Stoughton.

GRIMSBY COLLEGE
LIBRARY
NUNS CORNER, GRIMSBY